CNA and Caregivers

Caring For a Dying Patient

Brenda Vickers Johnson

Independent Nurse Consultant and Educator

KE'ED publishing

Keeping everyone enjoying development

CNA and Caregivers
Caring For a Dying Patient

First Edition
by Brenda L. (Vickers) Johnson

Assistant to the Author

Doretha Bell

Copy Editor

Paul W. Conant

Marketing Director

Larry Johnson Jr.

Marketing Coordinators

Cynthia Johnson Hester

Assistant to Marketing Coordinator

Theola Anderson

Illustrators

Cody Bednarz
Tony Jimenez

Cover Design Coordinator

Johnny Castanon

Cover Art Coordinator

Debbie Gabel

Reviewers and Consultants

John Berg, MS, BS, LNIA Administrator
Barbara Council, RN, PCI Program Director
Sharon Johns, BSN, RN, Director of Nursing
Ollie McCormick, LVN
Velma Rhue, LVN
Bishop David L. Robinson
Rev. Mary Schumann
Dr. Jacquita Vickers
Myrtle Tolbert, 83-year-old Senior
Tommie, 85-year-old Senior
Ginny, 88-year-old Senior
Paul W. Conant, Copy Editor and 65-year-old Senior

Library of Congress Control Number:

Printed in the United States of America

ISBN 13:978-1491066430
ISBN 10:1491066431

NOTICE TO READERS

The purpose of this book is to provide the reader with information on what to look for with regard to symptoms that a dying person exhibits, and how to care for that dying patient. Since each death is unique, this book can only give the reader ideas and helpful tips to consider. It does not claim to have all the answers.

This book does not offer medical advice to the reader, and is not intended as a substitute for appropriate health care and treatment. For such advice, readers should consult a licensed physician. For psychological/emotional advice, consult a psychiatrist, psychologist or spiritual advisor. For spiritual advice, consult a pastor, priest, rabbi, chaplain or spiritual advisor. For an individualized care plan designed just for your patient or loved one, consult with the Facility Nurse. If the patient is in the home, consult with the Hospice Case Manager, but if the patient is not on hospice, consult with the patient's doctor.

This book addresses the physical and emotional aspects of dying and should be used as one source of information concerning how to care for a dying patient.

Because this particular version was written for School use, the spiritual information is limited to the grieving process and how to communicate with the patient and family members.

Table of Contents

Table of Contents (continued)

Endorsements

"The *CNA and Caregivers Caring For a Dying Patient* breaks the barrier and gets to the point of patient care."

–John Berg, MS, BS, LNFA, Administrator

CNA and Caregivers Caring For a Dying Patient, I realized how effective this material will be for the caregiver, and the patient who is going through the natural process of dying. There are key elements that each person who is involved with those last precious moments should be aware of in order to make it a "good death," and this text covered it thoroughly and understandably. I enjoyed it and am excited to know that someone has made the much-needed information available."

–Sharon Johns, BSN, RN, Director of Nursing

"The *CNA and Caregivers Caring For a Dying Patient* was very informative to me personally, being a CNA myself. It was so clear and concise. I think this book is a must read for every CNA."

–Karen Black, CNA

As an experienced hospice nurse, I highly recommend *CNA and Caregivers Caring For a Dying Patient* as a much-needed resource for every CNA caregiver. Without reservation, I sincerely encourage each CNA to keep a copy of this important reference near at hand."

–Terri Dobbs, LVN

"This is a great teaching tool for not only nursing assistants, but anyone who has to take care of a dying person. Being in the teaching profession of Nursing Assistants / PCT (Patient Care Techs) at PCI Health Training Center, I fully endorse that this manual will be a great asset to any health training professional."

–Barbara Council, RN, Program Director

Senior Endorsements

As a person ages into his or her senior years, they are often faced with the death of a spouse, sibling, close friend, or someone else of their own generation. Naturally, this makes them wonder about what will happen when they are at the end of their own life. Any senior will benefit from reading this book. The *CNA and Caregivers Caring For a Dying Patient* also has endorsements of Seniors.

"Brenda, as I read your book, I realized how helpful it is. You have made the world aware of what to expect and what to do at a difficult time in their lives. This will certainly help me prepare for my own death."

–Myrtle Tolbert, 83, Dallas, TX

"As a Senior Citizen that has more yesterdays than I do tomorrows, I was very impressed with *CNA and Caregivers Caring For a Dying Patient*. It gave me insight and hope that I will be blessed enough to have such a compassionate "friend" to help me and my family make that ultimate transition an easy one."

–Tommie, 85, Mesquite, TX

"God bless you, Brenda! After reading your book and knowing how you care for your patients, I feel my family and I will have that special person to help us prepare for the end of life on this earth. Thank you."

–Ginny, 88, Mesquite, TX

"Brenda, as I've studied your book and the upcoming PowerPoint presentation on this material, I keep thinking of more and more ways for people to benefit from understanding these concepts. The CNAs will be at a great advantage. Nurses and doctors will be jealous! Nursing home directors will want to make these available to the families of the residents that live there. Funeral directors will want to make these available to those who prepay their funeral expenses. You have learned so much from your experiences, and now you're sharing your knowledge in as succinct a way as possible with those that can benefit from it the most! I'm thankful to be able to learn all these things, and I'm going to make sure all my senior friends have access to this knowledge, too. To God be the glory!"

–Paul W. Conant, 64, Dallas, TX

Foreword

BJ has finally written a book! I can't wait to read it, and I hope this is the first of many. BJ is one of the most talented health-care providers I've had the honor to work with. Knowledgeable, compassionate, and a natural-born teacher all describe her. She relates well to all members of any team she works with, particularly those she shares her teaching skills with—CNAs, nurses, physicians, and especially families—and shares her unique ability to care physically, emotionally, and spiritually for the patient. She also has a terrific sense of humor! She loves her profession, and I'm fortunate to share her love of healing.

–Nancy Taylor, R.N., Hospice Case Manager

When my grandmother was dying, my family was so blessed to have excellent care from a wonderful nurse that had the knowledge/training covered in this book. That knowledge not only helped my grandmother have a comfortable and peaceful passing, but also helped me and my family through that process with her. Brenda was able to educate us along the way, so we knew what to expect as we went through the dying process with our loved one. Information/training of this type is much needed so that other families can have the kind of positive experience that we did. – Joy Wingo

"This is a 'must-have' book to help you through the process of the terminally ill patient." – Debby York, RN, Hospice Nurse

"The heart and compassion for the dying and their loved one is truly reflected in the teaching of the author." – Nancy Hutton, RN, Hospice Nurse

Acknowledgments

I thank God for teaching me how to care for my patients so that they could have a peaceful and comfortable transition to the other side. Thanks to my patients who individually taught me something new each time I had a case. I thank the many families who, in spite of their pain, welcomed me into their homes to care for their love ones. Thanks to my Pastor, Bishop David L. Robinson for telling me the truth even if the truth hurts. And I thank Doretha Bell, my typist and friend for over twenty years, always available even when she really wasn't, i.e., at work.

Thank you, Nicole Rincon at The Art Institute of Dallas for taking your time to listen to my desperate cry for artists and posting the job request for illustrators; many responded. Cody Bednarz, Debbie Gabel and Tony Jimenez were chosen for the job. They are some of the most skillful I've seen!

Thanks to my Dad, Joseph "Sonny" Vickers, my son, Larry, and my siblings: Jacquita, Bridgett, Jeff, Kim and Calvin, for your love, support and encouragement even when it looked like I had been writing *forever* with no results. A special thanks to Robyn Conant for telling me your husband is an editor and for the piece of paper that you wrote his name and phone number on. I placed it on the wall at eye level so when I sat at my desk I could see it. For two years, I thanked God for my editor before even calling him. Thanks to Paul Conant, for believing in my vision enough to start editing my material without pay, and still, until Christmas Eve, 2011, had never met me in person. I have learned and am still learning daily from your wisdom and expertise. Thank you for being patient with me even when I cause you to pull your hair out!

Bless you all!

Preface

When I attended CNA School, the only information we were taught concerning End-of-Life Care was what to do with the body after death. No information or teaching was done on how to care for a patient that's dying prior to taking their last breath.

Still, when I attended Nursing School, there was no information in our books about how to care for a dying patient. When a patient is actively dying, they need specialized care according to their own unique way of transitioning through the dying process. It is different for each person; while they may have some similarities, no death is the same.

The *CNA and Caregivers Caring For a Dying Patient* will help anyone caring for a person dying to be more sensitive to the potential discomforts and anticipate how he/she might handle a situation before it occurs.

The *CNA and Caregivers Caring For a Dying Patient* was written to train CNAs and caregivers to know what signs and symptoms of discomfort to expect when caring for a dying patient.

In the beginning of the *CNA and Caregivers Caring For a Dying Patient* is listed simple tasks that a CNA or any caregiver can do to help a dying patient be and stay comfortable, resulting in a peaceful transition.

How you communicate with your patient affects your patient's comfort level. The *CNA and Caregivers Caring For a Dying Patient* will teach the reader not only how to communicate with the patient, but with the family also.

Often, the dying person's roommate is overlooked. Included in the *CNA and Caregivers Caring For a Dying Patient* is what to look for in the roommate. They grieve, too!

There are two words used in this book that normally a CNA would not be familiar with, i.e., *moribund* and *Hippocratic Facies*. If you have cared for a dying person, you have witnessed what they mean in changes that occur during the dying process. The two words are related; the first word means dying, and the latter one describes how a dying person might look.

The chapters on Body System Changes will give the reader a quick reference to common changes seen when caring for a dying person; e.g., the Cardiovascular System, the Gastrointestinal System, etc.

In the back of the *CNA and Caregivers Caring For a Dying Patient* are Frequently Asked Questions by CNAs and the author's responses. You will also find a CNA's Personal Loss History (as an Appendix) to use to get in touch with your own feelings concerning death and to equip you emotionally to be better able to care for your patient, and a reminder of ethical and legal issues a CNA should already be familiar with.

Because each individual person is unique, there may be signs and symptoms that may occur in your patient that are not mentioned. The *CNA and Caregivers Caring For a Dying Patient* does not have all the answers concerning how to care for a dying patient, but it will provide a foundation that the reader can build upon while performing the specialized care needed for someone dying.

Depending on the location of the dying person, the term referring to that person will change. For example, in nursing homes or long-term rehab facilities, assistant living facilities and retirement homes, the dying person will be referred to as *resident*. Some home health agencies and group homes refer to the dying person as *client*. In hospitals, hospices and doctor's offices, the dying person is referred to as *patient*. Also, the *CNA and Caregivers Caring For a Dying Patient* refers to the dying person as *patient*. Death is not an easy topic for most people, but it is a part of life that we all will experience one day. *–Brenda L. Johnson*

Introduction

Certified Nurses Assistants (CNAs) and Caregivers are the backbone of patient care. Your coworkers, dieticians, maintenance workers, D.O.N.'s, charge nurses, administrators, doctors, outside services like home health and hospices, including family members, all depend on you. Without you the team suffers.

End of Life Care

The team's main goals are to treat each patient with dignity and to keep the patient comfortable. The CNAs and **All** Caregivers are the first line of contact on a daily basis with the patient to make these goals happen.

How?

- By communicating with the patient.
- By recognizing signs and symptoms of discomfort.
- By providing good hygiene care.
- By recognizing and respecting when the patient's appetite changes.
- By communicating with the family.
- By recognizing moribund changes.
- By keeping patient in proper body alignment.
- By respecting spiritual/cultural beliefs that may be different from your own.
- By providing postmortem care.
- By being aware of your own feelings and emotions.
- By reporting promptly to your nurse the patient's discomfort/concerns.

CHAPTER ONE

<u>Communicating with a Dying Patient</u>

Speak in a slow, calm voice. Introduce yourself.

Explain to the patient what you are getting ready to do.

Allow the patient a few seconds between you telling them what you are going to do and you're actually performing the task.

- If the patient is still able to communicate and refuses care, remember he/she have rights. Report situation to your nurse.

- If you are a family member taking care of a loved one, do not stress and make a big deal about refusal of care. Try later and remember everything do not have to be done on a routine basis anymore. Always be respectful in tone of voice communication is both verbal and nonverbal.

- Being aware of cultural differences will help you better to understand, communicate, and provide individualized care for your patient/loved one.

How does a dying patient communicate?

VERBAL

One or two words

Slow speech and long pauses

Low weak voice

Demanding angry voice

Normal speech pattern (rare)

NON VERBAL

Creative gestures (primary caregiver usually understands)

Facial communication (raise an eyebrow, mouthing, facial grimacing)

A smile

Blinking eyelids or squeezing eyelids

A touch, squeezing a hand

Holding a hand, a change in respirations

Squeezing a fist (usually indicate pain or discomfort)

Physiological and emotional

Upper and lower extremity movement

Unseen

Sometimes they talk to the unseen

Make facial expressions

Reach out for someone they see

Spirit to spirit

CHAPTER TWO

<u>Recognizing Signs and Symptoms of Pain</u>

Signs and symptoms to look for:

- The patient states he/she is in pain or having pain.

- The family says the patient is in pain or having pain.

- The following can occur (with or without the patient having pain, but are the most common indicators of pain):

- Clenching his/her fist

- Moaning

- Making facial grimacing (frowning)

- Exhibiting shortness of breath

- Having labored breathing

- Agitation

- Restlessness, anxiety

- Elevated blood pressure

- Rapid heart rate

- Crying

- Difficulty sleeping

- Loss of appetite (patients do not want food when in pain)

- Dehydration is a contributor to the patient's pain due to the excess water loss from the body; therefore, the nerves are not cushioned by hydration. Remember, our bodies are composed of 60 – 70% water.

There are other signs/symptoms that may be unique to the individual patient.

Recognizing Signs and Symptoms of Pain (continued)

How the CNA Can Help

- If patient is able to respond, ask the patient if he/she is in pain or having pain.
- Observe patient for facial grimacing or moaning.
- Reposition patient every two hours if tolerated (see turn or not to turn chapter on repositioning patient).
- Sometimes the pain or discomfort is from being in one place for a period of time and there is no way of really knowing if the pain is positional related until patient is repositioned.
- If possible try to reposition patient prior to going to tell the nurse, unless a call light is at your fingertips; In that case let your nurse know immediately that patient is in pain then gently reposition patient for comfort. If there is no call light, reposition the patient first before going to tell the nurse.
- Always use pillows or foam for support of extremities and bony areas.
- Make sure patient is in proper body alignment.
- Check to see if linen is clean and wrinkle free.
- Each patient is different what works for one may not work for another.
- Since patient is usually not verbally able to tell us if they are in pain, or not; we have to rely on our senses.
- Be sensitive.
- Get to know your patients. Be observant each time you enter your patient's room.
- Report discomfort/observations to nurse.

CHAPTER THREE

Recognizing Signs and Symptoms of Respiratory Distress

Signs and symptoms to look for:

- Shortness of Breath (SOB)

- Labored breathing

- Cheyne-Stokes Respirations

- Rapid breathing

The following can occur with or without the patient having respiratory distress:

- Discoloration of skin, i.e. lips/nail beds pale to purplish
- Perspiring
- Mouth breathing
- Death Rattle: a rattling or gurgling sound due to loss of cough reflex (hearing the death rattle doesn't necessarily mean the patient is experiencing discomfort; usually the death rattle causes more distress for the family and caregivers than the patient).

How the CNA Can Help

Make sure patient is in proper body alignment.

If patient is on oxygen, check tubing to ensure it is not under patient or kinked.

It is okay to check to see if oxygen is on and how much (do not change dial).

At the end of life, the patient is either on room air or oxygen. The best method of delivery for oxygen (when the body is shutting down) is room air or nasal cannula. Most patients can and do tolerate oxygen by face mask up until they start fighting the mask (What is fighting the mask? increased shortness of breath and labored breathing or using chest and abdominal muscles to breathe with the face mask on). Once the patient's respirations are shallow, the carbon dioxide (CO_2) level in the body increases. The face mask at this point usually causes respiratory distress and needs to be changed out to nasal cannula or no oxygen at all. As the patient loses the ability to blow off CO_2, instead of decreasing respiratory distress, oxygen delivered by face mask at **this** point usually increases respiratory distress resulting in discomfort for the patient. Report discomfort/observations to nurse.

Warning   Warning

If the patient or your loved one lungs are already wet, or when they cough you can hear congestion in their lungs, They **Do Not** need humidified air. Please let the nurse know that the patient's lungs are wet or that you hear congestion; if you hear the death rattle, the patient **Do Not** Need humidified air. As a person transition through the dying process, the caregiver should anticipate what usually happen as the body shut down and be proactive rather than reactive. The following are the most common discomforts that occur at end of life that involves the patient's airway: Respiratory Distress, Shortness of Breath, Air Hunger, Agonal Breathing, Apnea, one or both lungs filled with fluids. A person can experience all of the above, a combination of the above or none of the above. A person that does not experience any of the above signs or one or two is usually a person that has been medicated on a regular basis prior to any obvious respiratory distress. As a CNA, all you can do is report signs and symptoms to the nurse. Sometimes repositioning the person helps to resolve the problem. If you are a family caregiver administer medications as ordered and then notify nurse/doctor if medications do not provide comfort.

If a person has history of smoking, diagnosed with lung cancer, COPD or any lung disease, they usually will experience respiratory distress; just knowing their history would help a nurse or caregiver anticipate that they may not benefit from humidified air. Staying in front of the curve when it comes to managing a dying person's symptoms is far better than trying to catch up after they are in distress. As a person transition toward crossing over their needs change as their body shut down. Dying is a transitional journey as a person get closer to their last breath, they no longer need what they use to need because they are leaving this world. The goal is to keep the patient comfortable. Be open to change.

CHAPTER FOUR

Recognizing Signs and Symptoms of Restlessness/Anxiety

Signs and symptoms to look for:

- Labored breathing
- Facial grimacing
- Moaning
- Raising shoulder

- Head or body movement
- Rapid heart rate
- Elevated blood pressure
- Others

How the CNA Can Help

Observe the patient's environment; a dying person's environment can contribute to restlessness and anxiety for example:

- Room too hot or cold.
- Overstimulation:

  o T.V./Radio too loud

  o Loud conversations around bed

  o Family conflict

  o Excessive rubbing of patient's body `

  o Too many people in room

o Strong colognes or perfumes
Report discomfort/observations to nurse.

CHAPTER FIVE

<u>Specialized Hygiene Needs of the Dying Patient</u>

Good oral care (most neglected):

- Gather supplies – toothbrush, toothpaste ½ glass of water with 1 or 2 caps of mouthwash if possible.

- Tell the patient what you are getting ready to do.

- Put on your gloves apply a thin layer of toothpaste.

- Brush the patient's teeth with a real toothbrush, **not** a mouth swab.

- Place your index finger in the patient's mouth between the outer wall of teeth and jaw line, exposing teeth and gums.

- Gently brush patient's teeth, small areas at a time. Rinse toothbrush in water.

- Use a mouth swab to remove excess toothpaste and to keep mouth moist.

Gentle bed bath/partial bath (as long as patient can tolerate it).

Good pericare (keep patient clean, dry, and comfortable).

Apply lotion/skin barrier (to soothe and protect skin).

If the patient has a bedsore or decubitus, or needs a dressing change, please let your nurse know that you are getting ready to bathe the patient so that treatment can be done at the same time.

<u>Notes—Strong-smelling lotions/perfumes may agitate patient at end of life.</u>

<u>Universal precaution should be used anytime you care for residents.</u> *

<u>Questions:</u>

1. What is the largest organ of the body?

2. What organ is a water-resistant barrier?

3. What organ protects all organs and skeletal muscular systems?

<u>Answers:</u>   1.–3. Skin.

CHAPTER SIX

Recognizing Moribund Changes

Moribund—in a dying condition; dying.

Changes to look for:

- Acetone breath (fruity breath)
- Mouth breathing
- Change in breathing pattern
- Increased apnea (longer pauses in breathing)
- Elevated temperature (above 100.3)
- Abnormally low temperature (below 96.5)
- Eyes closed or open and fixed
- Unfocused eyes
- Impaired speech
- Loss of movement/muscle tone
- Inability to arouse patient
- Severely unresponsive state
- Mottling (a purplish or blotchy-red discoloration of the skin)
- Others

*Be sure to report changes to the nurse.

Hippocratic Facies—the appearance of the face, felt in ancient times to indicate death was imminent. ***Today in the 21st Century, Hippocratic Facies is still such an indicator.***

Characterized by:

- Dark brown, livid or lead-colored skin
- Hollowed appearance of the eyes
- Collapse of the temples
- Sharpness of the nose
- Shallow facial expression
- Concavity of cheeks

CHAPTER SEVEN

<u>To Turn or Not to Turn</u>

The rule is to turn a patient every two hours—some facilities do it every hour. We do it without taking into consideration that at end of life the patient is severely dehydrated. Movement—sometimes just a light touch—can cause pain and discomfort.

- Turning a patient that's **actively** dying sometimes interferes with the patient's comfort especially if the patient is already relaxed showing no signs of discomfort. A tilt is more comfortable than a turn.

Factors that can delay or interfere with a patient dying a peaceful death:

- Worrying
- Pain
- Unfinished business
- Room too hot
- Force-feeding patient
- Anxiety
- Family conflict
- Too noisy
- Respiratory distress
- Unforgiveness
- Rough handling of the patient and not telling the patient what you are getting ready to do
- Others

However, the number one cause of delay in the dying process is the patient's will. Patient is not ready to "Go".

The number two cause is the family's will. The family being very emotional and is having a hard time giving the patient permission to "Go".

For example, a family member may insist the patient have a bed bath at a time when the patient is completely comfortable but very close to transitioning. The stimulation from rubbing on patient's body increase heart rate, respirations and pain contributing to anxiety making it difficult for patient to relax and let "Go".

Or family insists that the patient need water or something to eat when patient is no longer able to swallow. Sometimes the family have a need to try to feed their loved one themselves in order to understand they can no longer swallow. The family is with-in their rights to try. Let your nurse know what's going on.

<u>To Turn or Not to Turn (continued)</u>

Another example would be when some family members insist that their loved one be turned every 2 hours regardless of the discomfort it causes the patient or how close the patient is to their last breath.

The patient at this point is not aware of the flesh, and the turning is done to make the family feel better, disregarding what's really best for the dying patient.

In addition, if the patient's lungs are filling with fluids, sometimes turning a patient at this point causes respiratory distress, anxiety and pain for the patient, due to redistribution of fluids in the lungs.

If a patient is turned to another position and is showing signs of discomfort, observe the patient for 5 to 10 minutes; if the patient is showing distress in the new position, reposition the patient even if it means turning him/her back to the original position.

Some families decide early on that they do not want their loved one turned unless the patient needs to be changed because they can see the discomfort turning or movement causes the patient.

Most of the time the families are really stressed and want to know what's best for their loved one; however, even when told, they often reject teaching because of grieving. Be patient. Let your charge nurse know what's going on.

The caregivers, CNAs, nurses, doctors, family and friends have the ability and discernment to change the routine plan of care when the routine tasks no longer cause comfort but discomfort for the patient. This is an act of love.

- A tilt is far better at end of life than a turn. Using a draw sheet, gently elevate one side of your patient just enough to place a pillow underneath the patient's hip to relieve pressure.

To Turn or Not to Turn (continued)

- Two or three hours later, remove pillow and place under the opposite hip.

- Moving a patient's arms or legs may be all the repositioning a patient can tolerate.

- Never argue with a family member concerning the above, or any other, topic.

- You may find yourself having to turn a patient at the family's request, knowing that turning causes pain, discomfort, respiratory distress, and sometimes a complete turn can even cause a patient to take their last breath.

- Keep in mind; it's their family, not yours.

Unfortunately, as a CNA/caregiver, you will observe family/friends attempting to comfort their loved one by attempting to feed them or give them something to drink when they are not able to swallow, rubbing on them, messaging their back or feet, because that's what they have done every time they visited, and the patient enjoyed it.

- As a patient gets closer to death their needs change.
- There are some families that, no matter what you tell them that's best for the patient, they will do what they want to do, regardless of teaching and that's okay.
- Be supportive and nonjudgmental.
- This family member/friend is having a difficult time letting go and will not receive someone telling or asking them not to do something that they have been doing every visit, because it now causes discomfort for their loved one.
- They are coming to terms with their impending lost the best way they know how be patient and respect their need.
- Try to understand and give emotional support.
- Report concerns and observations to nurse.

CHAPTER EIGHT

Body System Changes

Neurological System:

Signs and symptoms to look for:

- Change in LOC (level of consciousness)

- Disoriented

- Unresponsive

- Patient unable to make needs known

- Others

Note—Remember patient can hear/understand you, even if they cannot speak or respond.

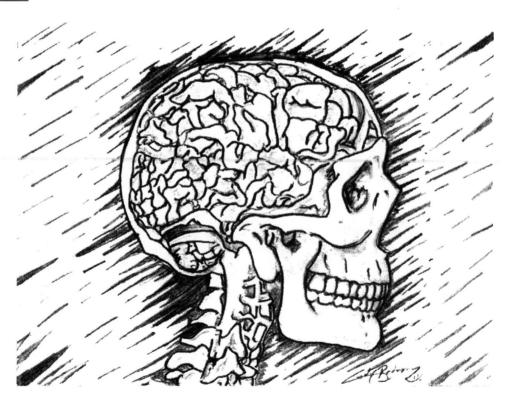

Body System Changes (continued)

Cardiovascular System:

Signs and symptoms to look for:

- Irregular heart rate/pulse

- Fast or slow heart rate/pulse

- Low blood pressure

- Blood pressure too low to register, yet patient is still alive

- Others

Body System Changes (continued)

Respiratory System:

Signs and symptoms to look for:

- SOB (shortness of breath)

- Labored breathing

- Apnea (short periods of no breathing)

- Congestion

- Death rattle (a rattling or gurgling sound due to fluid in the lungs and loss of cough reflex)

- Others

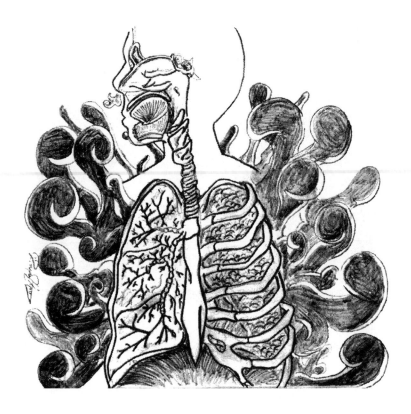

Body System Changes (continued)

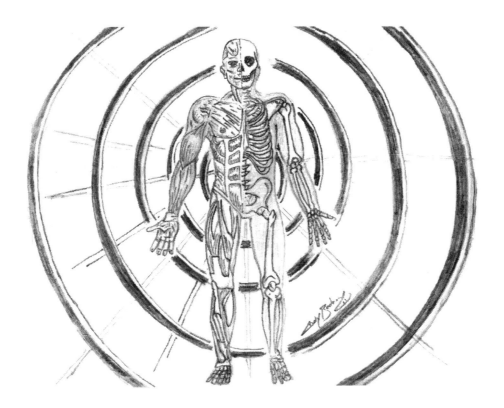

Musculoskeletal System:

Signs and symptoms to look for:

- Decreased mobility

- Stiffness

- Immobility

- Flaccidity (soft and limp; no muscle tone)

- Rigor Mortis (stiffening of the body <u>after</u> death)

- Others

Body System Changes (continued)

Gastrointestinal System:

Signs and symptoms to look for:

- Recognize and respect when the patient's appetite changes.

- Loss of appetite

- Dehydration occurs (also contributes to pain).

- The patient is not dying because he/she is not eating or drinking.

- Not eating/drinking is a symptom of the dying process.

- As the body shuts down, the need for food decreases.

- The body is unable to digest food.

- Eventually the patient is unable to swallow.

- Forcing food can cause patient to aspirate.

- Check for pocketing foods.

- Initially active bowel sounds

- Bowel sounds decrease.

- No bowel sounds

- No bowel movement

- Constipation

- Others

Body System Changes (continued)

Genitourinary System:

Signs and symptoms to look for:

- Incontinence (inability to control urination)

- Urine output decreases

- Urine color changes (usually to a dark tea color with a strong odor)

- No urine output

- Others

Body System Changes (continued)

Skin (Integumentary) System:

Signs and symptoms to look for:

- – Skin cool or cold

- – Low temperature

- – Skin hot to the touch

- – High temperature

- – Discoloration/mottling

- – Skin breakdown*

- – Others

CHAPTER NINE

<u>Respecting Spiritual/Cultural Beliefs</u>

Respect others

If the family wants you to pray with them or participate in their religious end-of-life practices, it is okay in their home; however, if you are in a facility be aware of the facility rules regarding this issue.

Some things the CNA/caregiver may hear from the patient include:
- Why is God making me suffer so?
- I just wish this were over.
- I can't stand it anymore.

As their CNA/caregiver, you can show you are empathic by:
- Acknowledging their suffering.
- Saying you are sorry, you don't have the answer or solution.
- Providing reassurance of your (or the team's) ongoing care.

Avoid any statements to family or friends that minimize the problem, such as "You must be relieved it is over."

Don't try to change their feelings.

Pay special attention to individuals who are not crying or demonstrating emotion. Just because they are not articulating their grief doesn't mean they are okay. Everyone who experiences loss needs our support, especially those who keep their emotions to themselves and have difficulty vocalizing their feelings.

Please report observations to nurse.

Notes

CHAPTER TEN

<u>Understanding the Grieving Process</u>

Grief is an emotional response to a loss:

- – A person
- – A relationship
- – A beloved pet
- – An opportunity or situation

Be aware of your own feelings/emotions.

Each person grieves in his/her own way.

Grieving starts before the patient dies.

Talk to someone about your feelings:

- – A coworker
- – A family member
- – A friend
- – A spiritual leader

Your care and concern for your patient expressed through nonverbal, verbal and written communication, makes you an essential link in the healing process.

Attend visitation or funeral if you are especially close with the family.

The grieving experience is not like any other experience; no matter how many times a person experiences it. It is different each time because relationships are different. With each of your patients or loved ones, you will grieve differently. Talk to someone about your feelings. Caring for someone on a daily bases creates a bond and sometimes a CNA is not aware of just how much he/she has bonded with the patient until the patient is on their deathbed.

Notes

Understanding the Grieving Process (continued)

Feelings and emotions that are common in grief include:

- Shock
- Anger
- Loneliness
- Depression
- Denial
- Being overwhelmed
- Disorientation
- Panic/Fear
- Rage
- Guilt
- Relief
- Isolation
- Sadness
- Regret
- Disappointment
- Others

Factors that may influence feelings and attitudes about death are:

- Your experience with death.
- Your personality type.
- Your religious beliefs.
- Your cultural background.
- Your ability to express your own feelings and communicate about death.

CHAPTER ELEVEN

<u>Communicating with Family</u>

Accept how the family grieves. (Don't be judgmental.)

Avoid "I know how you feel."

Do not rationalize the patient's death. E.g., "At least he/she is not suffering anymore."

Don't express pity when speaking with patient or patient's family.

Sometimes just be there quietly, with a hug or holding a hand, and it's okay to cry.

Ensure that you engage in:

- − Active listening.
- − Relaxed yet engaged body posture.
- − Eye contact (when culturally appropriate).
- − Reassuring touch (when culturally appropriate).
- − Listening beyond or beneath the literal words said by a person to the deeper emotions, meaning, and needs.

Do show that you genuinely care:

- − "We loved him/her, too."
- − "I will never forget him/her."
- − "We share your sorrow."

Information CNAs/caregivers can give families is limited. Know your scope of practice.

Communicating with Family (continued)

Additional ways CNA/caregivers can help:

_ Talking to the patient in a gentle calm voice letting them know what you are getting ready to do; not only comforts the patient, but the family also.

– By turning resident slowly and gently.

_ By asking the family if they would like something to drink.

– By being courteous and considerate.

– By touching to convey feelings when appropriate.

– By allowing the family to spend as much time as they wish with the patient.

– By allowing the family to participate in the care of the patient.

– By respecting their right to privacy.

– By communicating any request for clergy to the nurse or agency.

***Anything you do for the patient in front of the family is a form of communication to the family. Their emotions are very high and sometimes their perception is altered due to stress of losing their loved one, not eating , not sleeping, family conflict etc... Be observant and let your charge nurse know of any potential problems or concerns.

You are the eyes and ears for your charge nurse.

CHAPTER TWELVE

<u>Roommate Considerations</u>

When a dying patient has a roommate who may grieve as well, ideally the dying patient should be moved to a private room:

- It gives the patient and family privacy.

- It allows the roommate to remain in his/her familiar surroundings.

- It prevents the roommate from overhearing various discussions concerning the dying patient between employees, family and friends.

- It prevents the roommate from being disturbed from constant visitors in and out of the room, sometimes staying all night.

Signs and symptoms to watch for **in roommate:**

- Changes in normal habits, moods or vital signs. For example:

  o Crying

  o Sadness

  o Not eating

  o Fearfulness

  o Not sleeping

  o Rapid heart rate

  o Increased blood pressure

  o Staying out of the room

  o Angry
  o Others

Report discomfort/observations to nurse.

CHAPTER THIRTEEN

<u>Something to Think About</u>

- The patient is mouth breathing because he/she no longer has the strength or energy to keep his/her mouth closed.

- The person is snoring because their tongue is blocking his/her airway.

- The gurgling or death rattle is heard because of the buildup of secretions in the back of the throat or airway, and/or the loss of the cough reflex.

- Some people think that the patient doesn't know that he/she is dying. This is never the case, even if they have Alzheimer's, dementia, or a brain tumor, or are in a coma.

- It is our body that's giving out, wasting away, tired, aching, or is too cold or too hot, or has the illness or disease or pain; never the spirit and soul.

- Giving a person permission to "GO" makes letting go easier for the patient, contributing to a more comfortable transition.

- Often, we are very selfish when it comes to giving permission. After all, the people that is left behind—each individual—is only losing **one** person. But the person leaving has to detach from **all** that are left behind.

- A person on his/her deathbed learns a lot about the people they are leaving behind. Simply because he/she is not responding like they did the day before or not responding at all, makes it seem to the human mind that they are asleep or in a coma. Therefore, people do and say things they would not normally say or do in front of the person if they were up walking around.

Something to Think About

Over Stimulation

One of the problems in nursing homes is the night staff allowing the TV to be on all night; usually, the reason is the patient always had TV on, day and night. When a patient is on their deathbed, their needs change. A person that is dying needs quiet time, especially if they have had visitors all day.

Overstimulation can manifest itself mentally and physical in a dying patient. The various signs and symptoms a dying person encounters are intertwined. The process of elimination is key in assessing what works and doesn't work for a particular patient in order for them to be and stay comfortable.

Most of us are fearful about the unknown, but a dying person is often anxious, scared and sometimes angry on their deathbed.

A patient that is over-stimulated can appear to be restless, agitated, or in pain, or may experience respiratory distress or even a seizure.

Overstimulation can cause facial grimacing or moaning—two of the signs that indicate pain or discomfort in any patient, especially one dying.

Medication is usually given for these signs, but if patient is over-stimulated, removing the stimulation usually solves the problem; sometimes just turning the TV off or limiting the visitors for a while will allow the patient to get complete rest.

Giving medication for a man-made preventable stimulus just doesn't make sense; however, sometimes it's done especially if the family is unable to allow the patient the needed rest due to their own grieving process. Be empathic and allow the family what they need at this time. Keep your nurse informed of any and all issues concerning patient.

Something to Think About

The following is an example of a patient being over-stimulated, and how one might handle the problem:

A male patient was dying at home. There were kids running in and out of the room screaming and playing; there was a roomful of relatives and friends at bedside with 5 or 6 different conversations going on at one time; people were laughing and talking out loud; plus the TV was on. The day nurse had been medicating every hour because of signs and symptoms of the patient. She attempted to teach the visitors on overstimulation; however, they became hostile toward her and continued as they were prior to her saying anything. Once the night nurse arrived and got her shift report, she decided to speak with the patient's wife and daughter privately to explain about overstimulation and how the patient was being medicated but the meds were not helping. She explained all that he really needed was some quiet time. There were fifteen people in the room, not including the children that were running in and out. After getting support from the patient's wife and daughter, the night nurse was allowed to address the entire room at one time.

Keep in mind that everyone grieves differently and emotions are high at this time. Tone of voice and body language are being observed by 15 different people and most likely creating fifteen different interpretations of what's being said, which is why a CNA should report problems like the above example to their charge nurse.

The night nurse stated, "My name is Kathy, I will be caring for Mr. --- tonight. I know that this is a difficult time and you all want Mr. --- to be comfortable and pain–free." She paused for a few seconds to allow them to digest what she just said, then she continued: "In order for that to happen, he needs some quiet time for 2 or 3 hours without the TV on and without multiple conversations at bedside." A few people got a little upset about leaving the room, but they did. Within 20 minutes the patient no longer showed signs of discomfort. Everyone stayed out of the room for at least 2 hours. When they did come back to bedside it was 2 at a time for five or ten minutes.

As a CNA observing the patient for overstimulation, do not try to teach on the subject unless you are asked a particular question. Keep in mind that this is a very stressful time for the family. You are not expected to handle this type of situation nor should you try. Your charge nurse is the "go to" person for all problems and concerns.

<u>Your observations concerning your patients are important. Your charge nurse is depending on you.</u>

__Something to Think About__

Your Attitude

- ❖ 1. A negative attitude is not productive.
- ❖ 2. Hanging around negative people is not productive.
- ❖ 3. Be on time.
- ❖ 4. Dress to impress; iron your uniform.
- ❖ 5. No loud perfumes. No excess jewelry.
- ❖ 6. Don't do anything in a patient's room or anywhere you don't want caught on camera.
- ❖ 7. Your patients used to be able to care for themselves, now they can't. They, their families and facility depend on you.
- ❖ 8. Think about how you want to be treated if you were in that bed or how you would want your mother or grandmother to be treated.
- ❖ 9. A positive attitude in the workplace will affect everyone around you even if they have a negative attitude.
- ❖ 10. Be professional

Notes

Notes

CHAPTER FOURTEEN

<u>Providing Postmortem Care</u>

<u>Postmortem</u>—performed after death (care of the body after the patient dies):

- Close patient's eyes.
- Allow family time at bedside.
- Check with the family to make sure it's okay to do postmortem care.
- Find out if family has a special outfit for the patient to wear.
- In some religions, the patient is not touched after death, or there is a certain ceremony before postmortem care can be done.
- Then ask the family to step out of the room (or allow family member(s) to participate in postmortem care, if requested) while you:
  - o Sponge patient.
  - o Put on a clean diaper.
  - o If patient has a foley catheter, empty the BSB (some funeral homes prefer catheter to remain in place; check with your nurse).
  - o Put on clean gown or special outfit.
  - o Brush teeth (with a real toothbrush and toothpaste to remove buildup and food particles, mouth swabs will not remove. Do not brush gums too hard as this may cause bleeding.).
  - o Use a moist 4x4 gauze to remove toothpaste after brushing teeth.
  - o Look in patient's mouth to make sure there is no food particles or secretions in back of throat.
  - o Put in dentures if instructed by nurse.
  - o If patient has no teeth, use a moist 4x4 gauze to clean mouth and gums.
  - o Shave patient if needed (okay to apply after shave or cologne if patient normally wears it).
  - o Apply lotion.
  - o Comb hair.
  - o Ensure proper body alignment. (Place arms at sides, hands palms down or folded across abdomen.)

Providing Postmortem Care (continued)

- o Check to make sure eyes are still closed after movement.
- o Raise bed to waist level.
- o Straighten room.
- o Empty trash.
- o If possible, open windows to air the room.

- Let family back in room.

* Notes—

1. Check with your nurse concerning removing any type of tubing from patient's body.
2. Follow facility policy on personal items.
3. Most facilities have specific policies on postmortem care. Know and follow your facility's policies.

Special Notes

Some families are concerned about the patient's mouth being open.

A. Sometimes a second pillow under patient's head is enough to cause chin to tuck and mouth to close.
B. Sometimes family wants a ribbon around chin and top of head to keep mouth closed.
C. When all else fails, explain to family that it is normal for mouth to be open due to a relaxed jaw. (This is why brushing the patient's teeth with a tooth brush is an important part of postmortem care).
D. If your patient **normally** wears make-up foundation lipstick perfume etc…, applying make-up or perfume usually provides comfort for the family.
E. When a family member ask to help with post mortem care, try assigning them the task of applying the make-up, polishing nails, styling the hair or shaving the face. (Once I had a patient that had a son who was a dentist. I asked him, did he want to clean his dad's teeth one last time? The comfort and closure that gave the son was obvious to everyone in the room).

CHAPTER FIFTEEN

<u>FAQs and Answers</u>

1. Should a patient dying be treated differently from a patient that's not? At a certain point, a dying patient is treated differently than a patient that is not dying; for example:

   ♥ Bathing a patient may cause respiratory distress/pain.

   ♥ Turning patient may cause respiratory distress/pain.

   ♥ Rubbing on patient (attempting to comfort) may cause respiratory distress/pain.

   ♥ Feeding patient may cause patient to aspirate.

   ** All patients should be treated with dignity and respect.**

2. Does the patient know that he/she is dying?

   ♥ <u>Yes.</u>

3. Why is death a difficult topic to discuss?

   ♥ We fear death.

   ♥ Don't understand death.

   ♥ Uncomfortable with the thought of our own death.

4. Is there such a thing as a "good/bad death"?

   ♥ <u>Yes.</u>

5. What are some things that contribute to a death being a "good death"?

   ♥ The family talking openly and honestly about death to the patient, other family members, and friends.

   ♥ The patient planned ahead for his/her death.

   ♥ Family members getting along with each other and the patient.

   ♥ Forgiving each other if need be.

   ♥ Letting the patient know that it is okay for them to "GO."

   ♥ Letting the patient know that the ones left behind will be okay.

FAQs and Answers (continued)

6. What are some things you, the CNA/Caregiver, could do to contribute to a patient's death being a "good death"?

   ♥ Talk to patient and tell her/him what you are getting ready to do before performing task.

   ♥ Moisten patient's mouth with mouth swab often (whenever turning or repositioning).

   ♥ Turn patient every two hours **if** he/she tolerates it without causing distress. (See chapter seven for additional considerations when it comes to turning or not to turn.)

   ♥ Keep patient clean and dry.

   ♥ Keep room quiet, clean and odor free.

   ♥ Sit quietly, holding patient's hand when you have time.

   ♥Treat the patient with dignity and respect.

7. What are some things that contribute to a patient's death being a "bad death"?

   ♥ Family conflict, unforgiveness.

   ♥ Family/patient not talking openly about pending death.

   ♥ Family thinking the patient doesn't know he/she is dying (therefore, talking to everyone about the pending death but the patient).

   ♥ Patient worrying about the people he/she is leaving behind.

   ♥ Patient not having closure, or having unresolved conflict.

8. What are some things that you, the CNA/Caregiver could avoid doing (to avoid contributing to a patient's death being a "bad death")?

   ♥ Not communicating with the patient prior to performing a task.

   ♥ Talking loud; having a bad attitude.

   ♥ Talking to a coworker about a patient as if the patient is not present.

   ♥ Not keeping patient clean and dry.

   ♥ Leaving the TV or radio on loud day and night: too much stimulation.

   ♥ Not treating the patient with dignity and respect.

9. What about a dying patient's hearing?

- ♥ The sense of hearing is present in the body all the way to the patient's last breath. In other words the hearing leaves with the soul.

- ♥ If you have ever had an out-of-body experience or have heard someone's account of their out-of-body experience, they always talk about what they saw and heard while out of the body.

10. Is the patient really seeing someone in the room that only he/she sees?

- ♥ Yes! (Not because the deceased person is back on this earth. The dying person is the one transitioning in and out of this realm to the next.)

- ♥ Therefore, if your patient is talking to someone you do not see, give respect and allow the patient to have his/her conversation.

- ♥ It is okay to engage in a conversation with the patient about who they see, instead of telling them that they do not see whomever. Try asking them:

  - What are they doing?

  - What do they have on?

  - Are they talking to you?

  - What are they saying?

- ♥ When you ask the above questions, be sensitive and speak in a low, calm voice.

- ♥ For example, if the patient states that they see their mother, then you might ask, "What is your mother doing?" or "What is your mother's name?"

- ♥ Listen patiently and allow time for the patient to answer questions.

Your conversation will be comforting to the patient and assist the patient with having closure and a peaceful transition.

11. What is hospice?

♥ Hospice is a philosophy of care and **not** a place. It can be provided in nursing home facilities, assisted living facilities, retirement homes, family home, patient's home or a homeless shelter in other words, Hospice can be provided anywhere the patient lives. The type of care that Hospice provides is called Palliative care.

• Palliative care is a specialized care for terminally ill patients.

• Palliative care is not about shortening the time the patient has left on this earth (a common misconception not only of CNAs and other caregivers but people in general.)

• Palliative care is focused on pain and symptom control.

• Palliative care is about providing comfort. The comfort medications help the patient achieve that goal through allowing the patient to relax so he/she can "let Go." (see comfort meds on next page)

• A common misconception and reason why people believe that the medications "killed the patient" or the patient is "over-medicated" is that once the comfort medications are started, the patient is able to relax and not be anxious.

• The truth is the patient is getting ready to transition over to the spirit world in order for that to happen. The spirit has to be in control to enter the spirit realm, meaning the patient has to be relaxed enough to let the cares of this world "Go."

♥ The Hospice team includes: Physicians, Registered Nurses, License Vocational Nurses, Home Health Aids, Social Workers, Volunteers, Chaplains and Bereavement Counselors.

♥ After the person expires, the Bereavement Counselors are available for the family to provide Psycho-Social and Spiritual support up to one year from the time the person expires.

12. Why are some patients on hospice and some are not?

   ♥ The patient or family does not want hospice services.

   ♥ The patient's diagnosis does not qualify for hospice.

   ♥ The diagnosis qualifies but the length of time the doctor estimates the patient has to live is longer than six months.

   ♥ Some people do not know about the services hospice provides.

   ♥ Very little or no education on the benefits of hospice not only for the patient but the family too.

   ♥ A difficult decision for the family.

   ♥ Family feeling guilty about putting their love one on service.

   ♥ Family in denial – not ready to "let Go." Or some might be ready, others are not.

13. What qualifies a person to continue hospice services when he/she lives longer than the diagnosing doctors initial estimates, which can be up to six months?

   ♥ There has to be a steady decline in the patient's health.

14. Who pays for hospice care?

   ♥ Private Pay

   ♥ Medicaid

   ♥ Medicare

   ♥ Insurance

15. Where is a dying patient's home?

   ♥ A dying patient often states, "I want to go Home." Most caregivers/family members reply, "You are already home." But the Home the patient is speaking of is not on this earth.

FAQs and Answers (continued)

Do the comfort meds enhance/speed up the dying process?

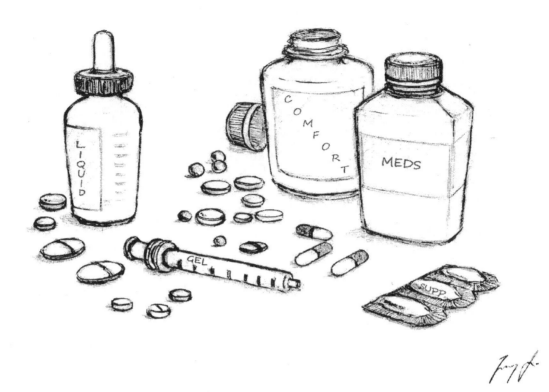

♥ Comfort meds do not enhance or speed up the patient's death; they help manage the signs and symptoms that occur during the normal process of dying. Comfort meds help the person relax so they can "GO."

♥ Increased pain, respiratory distress, anxiety, and fluids accumulating in the lungs are often what happen when the organs slow down and eventually shut down.

♥ Comfort meds help the patient to better tolerate such changes going on in the body (especially changes in the lungs) and remain relaxed and comfortable.

♥ For example, when a person takes a sedative or a sleeping pill, he/she can usually relax and go to sleep. So comfort meds help manage the patient's signs and symptoms, and help the patient to relax while the many changes are occurring within the body; although it does happen, it is very difficult for a person to transition in distress. If the medication does what its design to do, the patient will have a peaceful transition.

Review Questions

Certified Nurses Assistants (CNAs) work for:

- Skilled Nursing facilities
- Home Health agencies
- Rehabilitation facilities
- Hospices
- Hospitals
- Group Homes
- Doctor's offices
- Private duty (self-employed)
- Diagnostic Centers
- Staffing Agencies
- Other places

The questions below are based on skilled nursing facilities and bedside one-on-one private patient care within a CNA's scope of practice.

1. When a CNA is employed by a Skilled Nursing facility and is caring for a patient that is on Hospice, who does the CNA report a problem to first concerning the patient?

   a. Doctor   b. Hospice or other agency c. Family   d. Charge nurse

2. When a CNA is caring for a hospice patient one-on-one at bedside in the patient's home, who does the CNA report a problem to first concerning the patient?

   a. Doctor   b. Hospice or other agency c. Family   d. Charge nurse

3. Who does the CNA report a problem to next?

   a. Doctor   b. Hospice or other agency c. Family   d. Charge nurse

4. Whenever a CNA is at bedside in a hospice patient's home, this is the only time

   a CNA can give medication for the patient's comfort. a. True   b.   False

5. Sometimes when caring for a dying patient one-on-one in the patient's home, the CNA witnesses family stress due to the grieving process or for other reasons. Whom does the CNA notify first concerning the above issues?

    a. Doctor   b. Hospice or other agency c. Family   d. Charge nurse

6. Anything that a CNA observes that jeopardizes the patient's safety can be reported at the end of the CNA's shift to the Hospice or other agency.
    a. True   b. False

7. Anything that a CNA observes that jeopardizes the safety of the CNA is not important to the Hospice or other agency because the patient needs come first; do not report such situations because the CNA might not have a job after his/her shift!   a. True   b. False

8. A CNA (not employed by facility) is caring for a dying patient one-on-one at bedside in a Skilled Nursing facility. To whom is the first person a CNA reports a problem concerning a patient?

    a. Doctor   b. Hospice or other agency c. Family   d. Charge nurse

9. Who gets the second immediate notification of a problem?

    a. Doctor   b. Hospice or other agency c. Family   d. Charge nurse

10. List the four senses that a CNA uses to observe the patient:

    _____

    _____

    _____

    _____

11. What are signs and symptoms (referring to an illness)? _____

12. Why are signs and symptoms important concerning the patient? _____

    _____.

13. What does the term "objective data" mean? _____

14. What does the term "subjective data" mean? _____

15. The following statements are either subjective or objective data concerning any patient (dying or not). Place "S" for subjective or "O" for objective data concerning the patient:

a. _____ Patient is crying.

b. _____ Patient is sleeping a lot.

c. _____ Patient's urine is dark-tea color.

d. _____ Patient complains of pain.

e. _____ Patient's temperature is 100.7.

f. _____ Patient is coughing up blood.

g. _____ Patient's respiration is labored.

h. _____ Patient's nail beds and fingertips are deep red or purple in color.

i. _____ Patient is snoring.

j. _____ Patient's skin is moist.

k. _____ Patient states, "I am cold."

l. _____ Patient states, "I see my uncle standing at the foot of my bed." (No one else is in the room but the CNA and the patient.)

16. When a patient is actively dying, they can still hear.

        a. True   b. False

17. Because the patient is dying, the CNA can speak to the patient in any tone of voice. It doesn't matter at this point.   a. True b. False

18. List nonverbal ways a CNA can communicate to the patient.

_____

_____

_____

Review Answers

Special Note:

Some staffing agencies do not want the CNA to call directly to the hospice or home health agency when there is a problem in the **home** (after notifying the family). Some staffing agencies want to be notified second, and then they will immediately notify hospice or home health agency.

With other staffing agencies, it is okay for the CNA to notify the appropriate agency directly of problems in the home first, and then notify the staffing agency second.

It is important for the CNA to know and understand the expectations of the staffing agency for which they work. Usually there will be a folder or notebook at bedside showing whom to notify concerning problems that might occur.

1. d. When a CNA is working in a Skilled Nursing Facility always report problems to the Charge Nurse first, The Charge Nurse will report the problem to the appropriate agency. (You can also notify your agency after telling the Charge Nurse.)

2. c. Whenever a CNA is working one-on-one at bedside in a patient's home and identifies a problem concerning the patient, tell the family first.

3. b. After notifying the family of the problem, immediately notify the appropriate agency of the problem or concern. The phone number can be found in folder or notebook at bedside.

4. b. CNAs cannot give medication **ever**. Giving medications is outside a CNA's scope of practice. If it appears that the patient is experiencing pain, respiratory distress, restlessness or anxiety, tell the family member who can then administer medications.

5. b. Whenever any kind of conflict arises among family members and/or patient, always notify the Hospice or agency that assigned the CNA to the case. Do not try to resolve a family conflict. The agency will send a nurse, a social worker, a chaplain, or sometimes all three to help resolve issues within families.

6. b. Safety of the patient is of utmost importance. Anything that jeopardizes the patient's safety should be reported immediately to the hospice or agency that assigned the CNA to the case.

   For example: If the safety issue involves the family fighting verbally, notify the appropriate agency immediately.

   If the safety issue involves physical fighting among family members or is a life-and-death issue, **call 911**. Then immediately contact your agency.

   If the safety issue is that the bed is too close to the fireplace, notify the family first, and assist them if need be to move the bed away from the fireplace. Then notify the appropriate agency and document it.

7. b. If the CNA feels threatened or is in an unsafe environment, notify whomever assigned the CNA to the case immediately, unless it is a life or death situation, then **call 911 first** and get to a safe place.

8. d. When the CNA is not employed by the facility, but is caring for a patient in the facility at bedside, **always** notify the facility charge nurse first for any problem concerning the patient. If the problem is with the facility itself, e.g., the CNA reports to the charge nurse that the patient is in pain, and 30 minutes pass and the nurse has not come to assess the patient's pain; the CNA kindly reminds the charge nurse, but the charge nurse states, "Go sit down; I will get there when I have time." Immediately notify the agency of the problem.

9. b. When working in a facility in which the CNA is not employed, notify the hospice or other agency second of most problems (use common sense).

10. Hearing, seeing, touching, smelling.

Notes

Review Answers (continued)

11. Signs are what a CNA or Caregiver can see concerning the patient. Symptoms any changes in the body or its functions reported by the patient.

12. Signs and symptoms are important concerning a patient, because they are the means of helping the Doctors, Nurses, CNAs and Caregivers determine the status of the patient within their scope of practice.

13. Objective data are signs a CAN or Caregiver can see, hear, feel or smell concerning the patient or an observation the CNA/Caregiver makes concerning the patient.

14. Subjective data are symptoms the patient can convey to the CNA concerning how he/she is feeling. A CNA cannot observe the patient's symptoms.

15. a. O   b. O   c. O   d. S
    e. O   f. O   g. O   h. O
    i. O   j. O   k. S   l. S   .

16. a

17. b

18. The following are nonverbal ways a CNA can communicate with a patient:
a. Sign language.
b. In writing.
c. Posture:
  – The way a CNA sits.
  – The way a CNA stands.
  – The way a CNA walks.
d. A CNA nodding the head to indicate Yes or No.
e. Facial expressions:
  – Frowning.
  – Smiling.
f. The way a CNA looks at a patient.
g. Eye movement:
  – Rolling the eyes.
  – Not looking at the patient when talking to the patient.
h. A CNA's touch.   i. Others

Notes

Afterword

My writings address the deathbed experience. Usually the person has had a long illness; therefore, the people that will be left behind, as painful as it is to watch their loved one transition, still have time to prepare for the impending death; the dying person will have time as well to prepare on their deathbed. Not so with an unexpected or sudden death. The family or friends have no preparation time. This book doesn't speak to that type of death. On a person's deathbed, often time is wasted because the pain of losing someone is great. This time could be used communicating about real issues like your pain of losing them; or what you are going to do in the future like apologizing for something you did or said, forgiving a sibling or another family member for a wrong they'd done, or getting in touch with distance relatives or friends even though you don't like them to allow them to say their goodbyes; simply reminiscing about old times; respecting their spiritual beliefs, playing soft music at the bedside; or discussing funeral arrangements. All of these things facilitate closure not only for the dying person but for the ones left behind. Some people feel that talking about the funeral arrangements to the dying person or discussing it with the family in the same room of the dying person is disrespectful or will cause pain for the person. Actually, it is the exact opposite. The conversation is awkward for us, not the one leaving. They know that they are dying. Knowing what's going to be done or how things will be handled is comforting to the dying person, and it allows them to know that their loved ones are working through the process and will be all right. While each family member and friend has one person to let go, the dying person is lying there concerned about many people and has to detach from each person. Honest open communication assists the person in having a peaceful death.

Some people prepare for death and when that time comes they are ready; however, most of us feel when death comes it's forced upon us. We act as if it is foreign and we have never heard of it. It's easier just not to talk about it. But talk we must. Preparation brings comfort. Ignoring something that's a part of life doesn't make it go away.

—Brenda L. Johnson

Appendices

APPENDIX A: Personal Loss History

APPENDIX B: When I Die

APPENDIX C: The Dying Person's Bill of Rights

APPENDIX D: Ethical and Legal Issues

Personal Loss History

1) My first patient that died was _____ years old.

2) The first patient I ever witnessed take their last breath was (initials only) _____.

3) When I performed postmortem care for the first time, someone that had already experienced someone's death was with me to show me what to do.

   Circle   Yes   or   No.

4) After my first experience (performing postmortem care) I felt _____.

5) The way that I cope with the death of a patient is _____

   _____.

6) The way that I cope with the death of a family member is _____

   _____.

7) Do I feel a need to start preparing for my own death? Why or why not? _____

   _____.

8) Is there someone I need to ask to forgive me for something I did? _____.

9) The first death in my family was the death of _____.

10) My age was _____.

11) The death of _____ was the most difficult death I ever experienced.

12) What I believe happens when someone dies is _____.

13) Is there someone that I need to forgive? _____.

14) What would I like people to remember about me when I die? _____

   _____.

15) Name all the diseases my family members died from: _____.

16) For which am I at risk? _____.

17) What can I do to limit my risk? _____.

APPENDIX B

When I Die...

Name: _____ Date: _____

Burial Details:

_____ I want to be buried.
_____ I already have a cemetery plot at _____
_____ I do not have a cemetery plot yet.
_____ I want to be cremated and my ashes placed _____

Visitation:

_____ I would like my visitation service to be at _____
              _____ Funeral Home   _____ in my home   _____ does not matter
_____ I do not want a visitation service.

Funeral Home:

_____ I would like _____ Funeral Home to prepare me for burial.
_____ I would like my casket to be this color _____   _____ Color does not matter.
_____ I would like my clothes to be _____
_____ I would like my shoes to be   _____ on   _____ off
_____ I would like to have the following jewelry _____

Funeral Plans:

_____ I would like the time of my funeral to be _____
              _____ morning   _____ afternoon   _____ evening
_____ I would like the location of my funeral to be _____
              _____ at a church   _____ in my home   _____ at the graveside
_____ I do not want a funeral.

Funeral Service:

_____ I want the following included in my funeral service: _____
              Soloist/Musicians _____
              Songs _____
              Hymns _____
              Scripture Verses _____
              Other important elements _____
_____ I would like _____ to do my eulogy. (Alternative: _____)

www.keededu.org
© 2012 By Brenda Vickers Johnson

56

APPENDIX C

<u>Dying Person's Bill of Rights</u>

I have a right to:

- Be treated as a living human being until I die.

- Maintain a sense of hopefulness, however changing its focus may be.

- Be cared for by those who can maintain a sense of hopefulness, however changing this might be.

- Express my feelings and emotions about my approaching death in my own way.

- Participate in decisions concerning my care.

- Expect continuing medical and nursing attention even though "cure" goals must be changed to "comfort" goals.

- Not die alone.

- Be free from pain.

- Have my questions answered honestly.

- Not be deceived.

- Have help from and for my family in accepting my death.

- Die in peace and dignity.

- Retain my individuality and not be judged for my decisions, which may be contrary to the beliefs of others.

- Discuss and enlarge my religious and/or spiritual experiences, whatever these may mean to others.

- Expect that the sanctity of the human body will be respected after death.

- Be cared for by caring, sensitive, knowledgeable people who will attempt to understand my needs and will be able to gain some satisfaction in helping me face my death.

Source: Created at a workshop on "The Terminally Ill Patient and the Helping Person," sponsored by Southwestern Michigan In-service Education Council, and appeared in the *American Journal of Nursing*, Vol. 75, January, 1975, p. 99. Used by permission.

APPENDIX D

Ethical and Legal Issues

- Advance Directives—A legal document that allows people to choose what medical care they wish to have or not have if they become ill or disabled.

- The reason CPR is not performed on a patient in a facility is because the patient has a do-not-resuscitate (DNR) order.

- The reason CPR is not performed in a patient's home is that the patient or family member has signed a DNR form.

- Protected Health Information (PHI) states: Patient Information must be kept private.

- Never abuse a resident physically, psychologically, verbally or sexually.

- Watch for and report any signs of abuse or neglect immediately.

- There are two types of neglect:

  o Active neglect—purposefully harming a person by failing to provide needed care.

  o Passive neglect—unintentionally harming a person physically, mentally, or emotionally by failing to provide needed care.

- There are many types of abuse. Listed are only four:

  o Physical abuse refers to any treatment, intentional or not, that causes harm to a person's body. This includes slapping, bruising, cutting, burning, physically restraining, pushing, shoving, or even rough handling.

  o Psychological abuse is emotionally harming a person by threatening, scaring, humiliating, intimidating, isolating, insulting, or treating him or her as a child.

  o Verbal abuse involves the use of language, spoken or written, that threatens, embarrasses, or insults a person.

  o Sexual abuse is forcing a person to perform or participate in sexual acts against his or her will. This includes unwanted touching and exposing oneself to a person. It also includes sharing pornographic material.

Ethical and Legal Issues (continued)

– Negligence means action, or failure to act or provide the proper care for a resident that result in unintended injury.

– An example of negligence is a CNA forgetting to raise the side rail on bed after completing a bed bath; the patient rolls off the bed and is injured.

– Reporting abuse is the law. Failing to report means you participated in the abuse.

– Omnibus Budget Reconciliation Act (OBRA) has rules that are concerned with:

   o Requirements for nursing assistants.

   o Each resident's quality of life.

   o Safety regulations of health care facility.

– If you have questions or concerns regarding Ethical and Legal Issues:

   o Discuss with your charge nurse. If not resolved,

   o Discuss with your D.O.N. If not resolved,

   o Discuss with your Administrator. If not resolved,

   o Contact: Adult Protective Services

<u>References</u>

Hartman's Nursing Assistant Care—Long-Term Care and Home Health. Susan Alvare, Jetta Fuzy, RN, MS and Suzanne Rymer, MSTE, RN, C, LSW. © 2009, Hartman Publishing, Inc.

How to Say It by Jack Griffin and Robbie Miller Kaplan © 1994, Prentice Hall Press.

Mosby's Workbook for Long Term Care Assistants, 2nd edition. Relda Timmeney Kelly, RN, BSN, MSN © 1994, Mosby-Yearbook, Inc.

Taber's Cyclopedic Medical Dictionary, 19th edition © 2001 by F.A. Davis Company. [This refers to superscript in Ch. 6.]

Webster's II New College Dictionary © 2001, 1999, 1995 by Houghton Mifflin Company.

Notes

Notes

Made in the USA
Coppell, TX
20 October 2022

85021676R00042